AS IF KAREN NEEDS AN INTRODUCTION

Activity books are perfect for anyone who needs an escape from the real world. And between the demands of chauffeuring kids to and from practice, calling the police on probable illegals, and studiously ignoring science, no one is more entitled to a few moments of peace than the ultimate representative of today's most aggrieved, aggravated, and aggressive segment of the population: Karen.

It's a privilege to present this curated collection of activities that speak directly to every Karen's interests, regardless of how self-serving they may be.

So get a pencil, open a bottle of the peenogreege favored by your favorite celebrity Housewife, and get ready to spend some time finding solutions to many of the problems facing real Americans!

And if, for literally any reason at all, you *don't* enjoy this book, just go back to where you bought it, ask to speak to the manager, and demand a refund.

KAREN'S WORD SEARCH

```
W  E  Y  A  R  M  A  N  I  P  E  D  I  E  K  F  N  G  E
O  H  A  F  C  L  E  T  I  K  I  O  L  D  K  D  F  H  P
M  U  T  T  E  V  A  G  E  G  A  C  K  L  O  P  R  U  F
A  O  C  A  M  E  H  Y  I  N  S  T  A  W  O  R  T  H  Y
N  Y  C  O  P  A  G  A  J  O  F  A  C  M  F  I  I  J  L
A  O  R  S  M  N  M  U  G  S  M  F  G  F  F  B  D  N  N
G  I  C  T  A  P  P  B  U  O  E  F  C  K  E  E  I  I  U
E  I  Z  C  D  I  L  M  D  M  R  R  E  F  N  L  P  E  Y
R  G  G  I  H  Y  O  A  K  F  T  A  T  V  D  A  A  E  B
D  H  N  S  M  O  E  C  I  R  I  U  D  Q  E  G  N  N  W
O  R  I  P  E  N  M  F  P  N  G  L  E  E  D  E  I  T  B
X  C  N  E  P  P  I  E  N  D  T  A  L  N  E  N  B  I  C
U  A  E  H  J  I  N  R  S  Q  Y  O  G  A  P  A  N  T  S
C  P  O  M  P  T  I  O  N  C  M  Y  O  I  T  K  T  L  E
L  C  N  E  O  N  V  H  A  R  H  K  E  O  G  H  R  E  P
E  S  E  P  M  A  A  L  A  S  O  O  N  E  F  A  O  D  N
S  O  O  I  B  N  N  T  K  K  O  V  O  Q  A  R  P  I  E
I  A  N  S  K  O  M  E  T  Y  I  M  G  L  W  O  H  T  R
R  S  E  O  N  A  N  T  T  B  O  M  U  T  E  K  Y  S  O
```

nine one one   yoga pants
manager   minivan
instaworthy   homeschool
entitled   offended
manipedi   complaint

Answers on p. 98

I'D LIKE TO SPEAK TO THE MANAGER

Karen wants to return a dress she doesn't have a receipt for but wore only once.
Can you help her get to the Customer Service desk?

CUSTOMER
SERVICE

Answer on p. 98

PIN THE BLAME ON THE IMMIGRANT

Planning a neighborhood potluck is a lot like designing an immigration system. It all starts with a carefully curated guest list, one based on what each person is likely to bring, how they'll blend with the others present, and how much you think they'll take from the buffet. If all goes well you can trumpet yourself as the perfect hostess, but if something goes wrong, you'll need to quickly shift the responsibility to a scapegoat. Like Kevin Jr., who insisted on inviting his friend Mohammed. This fun game lets you have it both ways, as it perfectly combines passing the time and passing the buck!

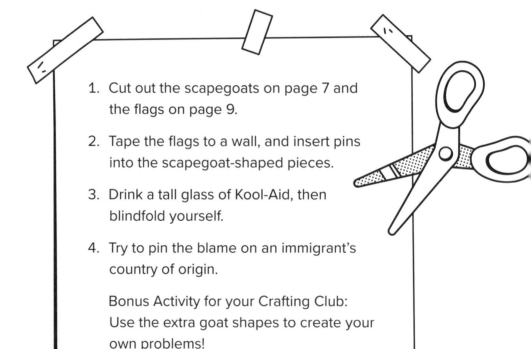

1. Cut out the scapegoats on page 7 and the flags on page 9.

2. Tape the flags to a wall, and insert pins into the scapegoat-shaped pieces.

3. Drink a tall glass of Kool-Aid, then blindfold yourself.

4. Try to pin the blame on an immigrant's country of origin.

   Bonus Activity for your Crafting Club: Use the extra goat shapes to create your own problems!

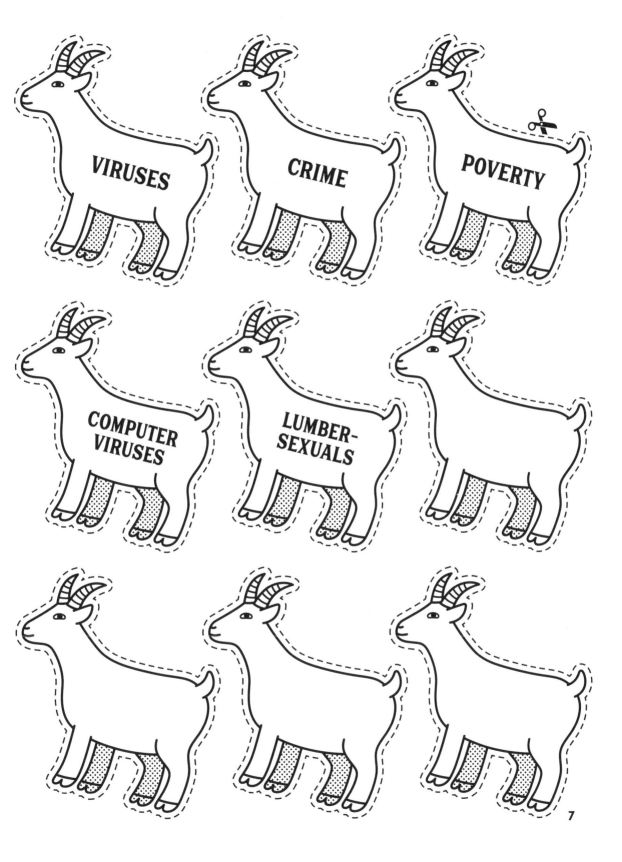

VIRUSES

CRIME

POVERTY

COMPUTER VIRUSES

LUMBER-SEXUALS

7

MEXICO

CHINA

CANADA

CONNECT THE DOTS...

to discover what NASA has been lying about!

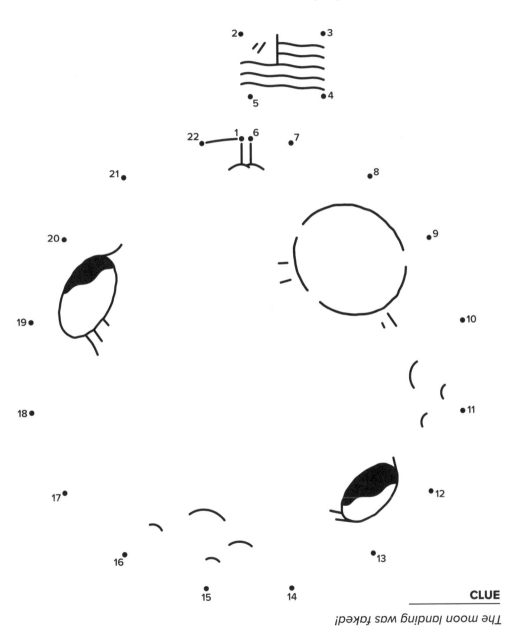

CLUE

The moon landing was faked!

Answer on p. 98

WHAT'S WRONG WITH THIS PICTURE?

A Day in the Park

CROSS-BITCH

Use this cross-stitch pattern to Karen-up your home!

EATING PARIS

Many people say the Paris of a theme park pavilion or Las Vegas hotel is just as good as the real thing. But the food in France is something special. Use these clues to name some of the most delicious venues in Gay Paree (just don't use that phrase in front of Kevin)!

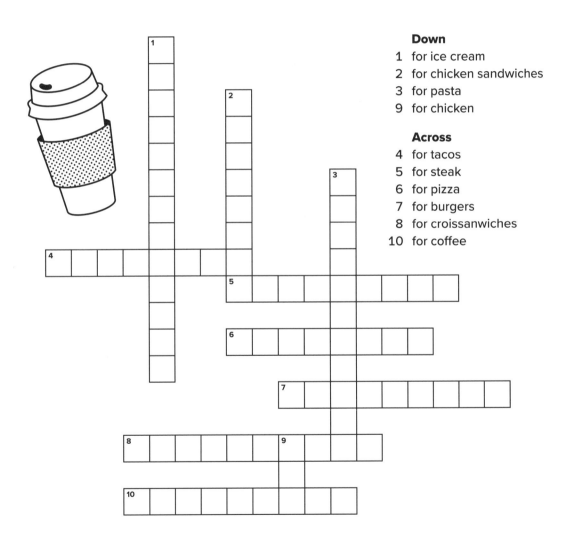

Down

1 for ice cream
2 for chicken sandwiches
3 for pasta
9 for chicken

Across

4 for tacos
5 for steak
6 for pizza
7 for burgers
8 for croissanwiches
10 for coffee

Answers on p. 98

IT BOGGLES THE MIND...

In today's mixed-up world, it's only natural for things to get a little confusing.
Unscramble your brain to decipher your rights!

THINGS YOU CAN'T TELL ME

Who to bake **kecas** for _____

How to **rpya** _____

Who to **ovle** _____

How to raise my **hindrecl** _____

What's **faes** _____

Where my **exsat** should go _____

Which **lgaf** to fly _____

What I can **ysa** _____

That my **pionino** doesn't matter _____

What to **earw** _____

THINGS I CAN TELL YOU

Who to bake **skace** for _____

How to **yapr** _____

Who to **velo** _____

How to raise your **drenilch** _____

What's **asef** _____

Where your **sxate** should go _____

Which **algf** to fly _____

What you can **asy** _____

That your **ninopoi** doesn't matter _____

What to **rewa** _____

Answers on p. 99

FAKE SCIENCE

Karen can clearly see, from the deck of her beach house,
that the horizon is flat. Can you help her navigate social media
as she finds and shares Flat-Earther posts?

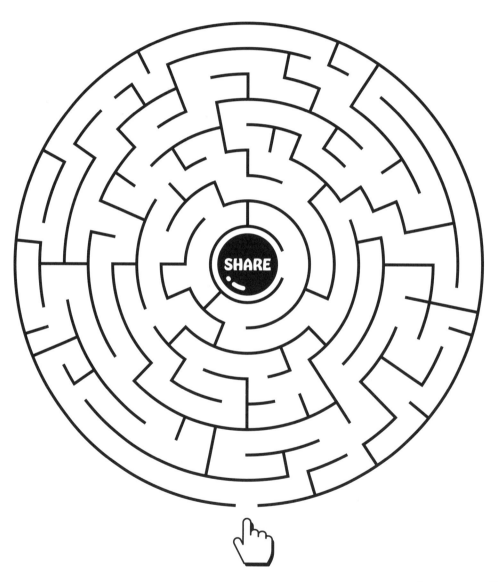

Answer on p. 99

CONNECT THE DOTS...

to discover what your doctor isn't telling you!

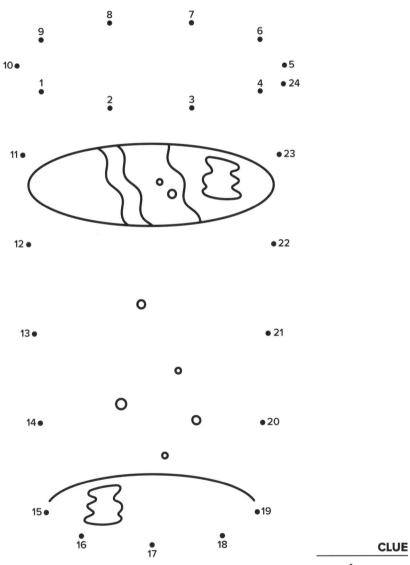

CLUE

Fluoride is put in your tap water to control your mind!

Answer on p. 99

WHAT WOULD KAREN DO?

Karen knows better than everyone else about everything and wants friends, family, and the world at large to think exactly like she does. But how best to convey the essence of what it truly is to Karen? Social media posts are all too easily flagged or reported, while yard signs and banners run the risk of insulting your sensitive snowflake neighbors. The best way to spread your views like so much mayonnaise on a ham sandwich is evidenced by the object you're holding in your hands: write and publish your very own book! Use the following pages to explain your way out of, and around, some common situations that every Karen faces. When you're done writing your manifestos, follow these easy steps:

1. Ask your child to help you connect your computer to the printer.

2. Print as many letter-sized copies as you think necessary to blanket your neighborhood. (Note: The A4 size on your printer is put there by Chinese bad actors to appeal to European deviants who want you to switch to the metric system.)

3. Cut along the dotted lines using a paper cutter or craft scissors (preferably purchased from a big box store that exercises its right to weigh in on their employees' health decisions).

4. Arrange the pages in order, with the pre-printed "WWKD?" cover at the bottom of the pile facing down.

5. Fold (do not cut) the stack of papers in half along the middle solid line. The "front cover" should read "WWKD?" and the "back cover" should have space for you to personalize it for gift-giving. (If you have trouble with this, ask your child to help. If they protest, remind them of all the tiny bricks you laid making their plantation diorama.)

6. Staple along the fold to keep everything in place.

7. Push your agenda into the hands and mailboxes of friends and family!

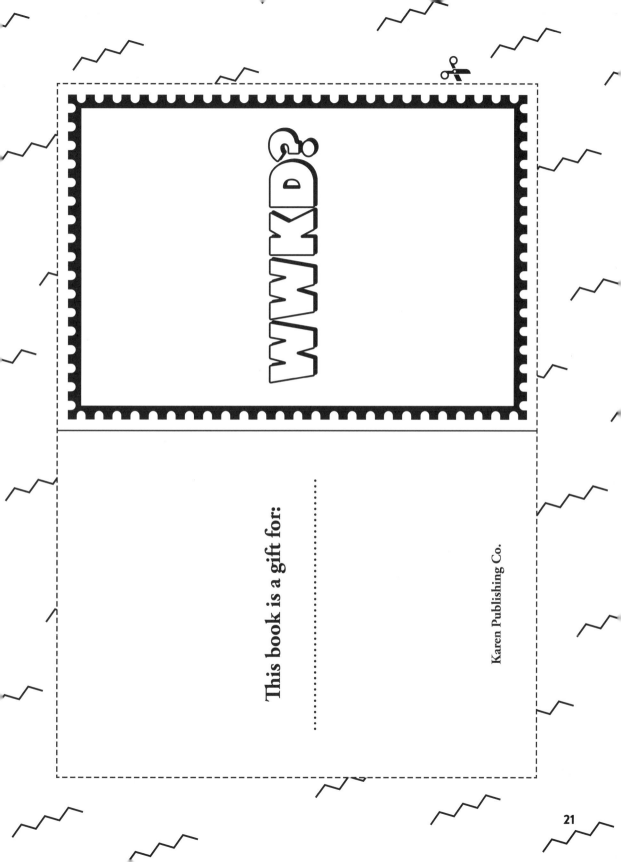

WWKD?

This book is a gift for:

....

Karen Publishing Co.

What to do when
you're mildly inconvenienced

What to do when
they won't let you speak
to the manager

What to do when
your neighbor has a
"Black Lives Matter" sign
on their lawn

What to do when you
can't get a pumpkin spice latte

What to do when
you enter a store 10 minutes
before closing

What to do when
your children aren't Insta-worthy

What to do when
your husband says "No"

What to do when
you're asked not to use the
word "Oriental"
for anything but a rug

What to do when
your child loses a sporting event

What to do when
nobody believes you have
black or gay friends

GIRLSQUAD!

Today's cliques are as diverse and inclusive as school districts, community standards, and good taste allow. Use these clues to uncover some of the unique names to be found in a modern #girlsquad!

Down

1 my daughter's friend
2 my daughter's friend
3 my daughter's friend
4 my daughter's friend
6 my daughter's friend
7 my daughter's friend

Across

5 my daughter's friend
6 my daughter's friend
7 my daughter
8 my daughter's friend

Answers on p. 99

RIDDLE ME THESE!

Q: Why is the *New York Times* like the theory of White Privilege?

A: Karen would never subscribe to either.

Q: How is Karen like Kevin's assault rifles?

A: They both have severe bangs.

Q: How is Fox News unlike Karen?

A: Kevin listens to Fox News.

Q: What's the only thing that scares Karen more than a Black man minding his own business?

A: A Black man owning his own business.

Q: How is a female colleague like a napkin?

A: Kevin would never have dinner with either of them without Karen present.

Q: How else is a female colleague like a napkin?

A: Both are employed to clean up Kevin's messes.

Q: How is a gay man like a handmade Father's Day gift?

A: Kevin would prefer they both stay in the closet and not be on display every June.

Q: How is the female orgasm like climate change?

A: Kevin doesn't believe in either.

WHAT'S WRONG WITH THIS PICTURE?

KEVIN'S WORD SEARCH

```
H  C  B  S  S  U  T  K  P  N  Z  V  B  E  C
N  A  S  K  E  T  M  M  A  N  U  P  R  A  X
B  M  O  P  T  R  U  C  K  P  O  S  O  W  P
S  O  P  D  S  A  D  T  C  L  O  J  M  L  N
O  V  U  K  F  V  H  Z  C  J  F  Q  L  K  C
N  P  E  G  O  T  Z  M  C  O  L  P  A  N  O
U  V  B  T  I  B  S  E  A  K  P  A  D  Y  D
E  F  H  D  A  I  B  V  R  N  E  D  K  F  Q
H  S  W  A  M  I  Q  R  G  M  C  Y  A  O  S
N  X  R  N  F  L  L  W  O  S  E  I  O  O  K
A  R  B  E  G  N  K  G  P  N  K  R  E  T  Z
N  A  B  E  P  L  G  I  A  O  H  D  K  B  E
B  S  Q  R  W  T  G  B  N  T  N  D  E  A  N
M  A  N  C  A  V  E  R  T  J  E  M  K  L  G
K  W  S  P  C  W  A  V  S  E  C  O  Z  L  S
```

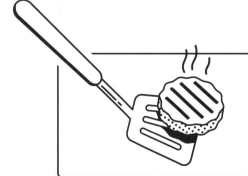

tailgate	truck
bbq	cargo pants
man cave	man up
football	camo
bro	

Answers on p. 100

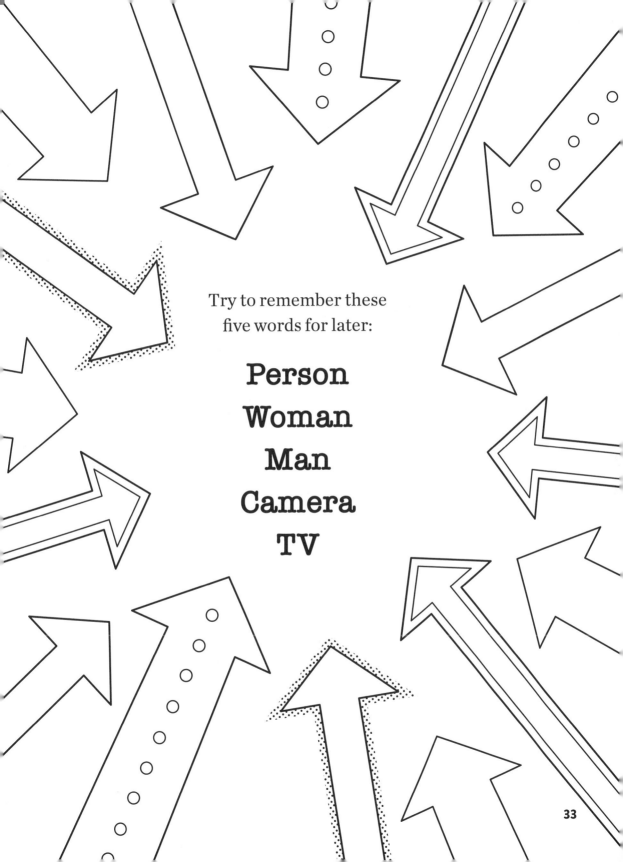

Try to remember these
five words for later:

Person

Woman

Man

Camera

TV

CONNECT THE DOTS...

to discover what Big Pharma doesn't want you to know!

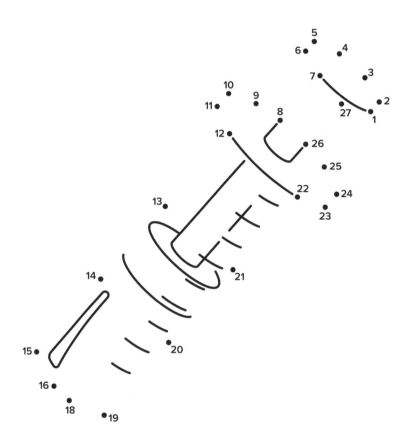

CLUE

Vaccinations cause autism!

Answer on p. 100

ALL-AMERICAN PAPER DOLLS

Color and cut out these pieces to play with your very own all-American family!

CROSS-BITCH

Use this cross-stitch pattern to Karen-up your home!

BOYS WILL BE BOYS!

To avoid having their lives ruined by pesky rape charges, boys need to be kept occupied. Like any good mother, Karen packs her son's schedule so full that he won't have the time or energy to get into trouble (not that it would be his fault if he did, of course!). Use these clues to discover some of the activities that keep Kevin Jr. on the right path.

Down

1 Saturdays 11am–1pm
2 Fridays 6pm–8pm
4 Mondays, Wednesdays, and Fridays 5pm–6pm

Across

3 Mondays and Wednesdays 7pm–9pm
5 Saturdays 8am–10am
6 Sundays 11am–1pm
7 Tuesdays and Thursdays 6:30pm–8pm

Answers on p. 100

MINIVAN MOM

Karen needs to pick up Kevin Jr. from soccer practice, Kayleigh from dance class, and Kevin from happy hour with the boys (so he doesn't get another DUI). Can you help her chauffeur her family home so she can finally relax with a bubble bath, a Xanax, and a copy of Ivanka Trump's memoir?

Answers on p. 100

DAM LIBS!

The mainstream media is always trying to put words in our mouths and distort what we mean. Fill in the blanks with your truth!

Hello, 911? My name is Karen. I'm feeling very _____
                                                  adjective
because a(n) _____ man is _____-ing near me.
                  adjective   verb

It's my right to say _____.
                            whatever

Go back to _____!
                non-European country

The _____ is true
            title of Good Book
because the _____ says it's true.
                same title of Good Book

I want to return this _____ I only
noun

used _____ times, but
number between 2 and 50

this _____ woman says I can't because I guess she
adjective

doesn't believe in _____.
traditional American value

I'm not _____.
adjective

Some of my best friends are _____.
plural noun

I support a woman's right to _____.
any verb but "choose"

I only tip the Uber driver if I think

he is _____.
documentation status

43

WHERE SHOULD THESE PEOPLE GO BACK TO?

SHE'S A GRAND OLD FLAG!

Use this rectangle to draw and color the American flag.
(Don't cheat by looking down at your shirt or around at your decor!)

Use this rectangle to draw and color what you think the American flag
should look like. (Get creative, and don't be cowed by the libs!)

Use this rectangle to draw and color your state's flag.
(If you'd forgotten states had flags, make up your own!)

Use this rectangle to draw and color what you are sure you saw
on an Antifa flag on the news or maybe Facebook (you don't remember
and don't have time to check, but it was definitely *somewhere*).

THOUGHTS FROM KAREN

Remember when you were young and kept a diary of your personal thoughts, hopes, and dreams? Whether you filled it with fantasies about your current boy band crush, vampire fanfic, or just a list of ways to get revenge on those who challenged your campaign for prom queen, a diary was a wonderful way to get your feelings out on paper, the better to later pin them to a vision board for actualization.

It's time to recapture the magic of a diary.

Use this space to list all the ways your neighbors violate the HOA guidelines.

Use this space to remember your favorite Girls' Night Out moments.

_____
_____
_____
_____
_____
_____
_____
_____
_____
_____
_____
_____
_____
_____
_____
_____
_____
_____
_____
_____
_____
_____
_____
_____
_____

Use this space to record all of the sacrifices you make.

Use this space to describe all the ways people should be allowed to protest.

_____

_____

_____

Use this space to describe all the ways people should not be allowed to protest.

_____

_____

_____

_____

_____

_____

_____

_____

_____

_____

_____

_____

_____

_____

Use this space to describe why you love America.

Use this space to get creative and draw all the Fourth of July outfits you could make out of an American flag.

Use this space to catalog your husband's faults.

_____

_____

_____

_____

_____

_____

_____

_____

_____

_____

_____

_____

_____

_____

_____

_____

_____

_____

_____

_____

_____

_____

_____

_____

Use this space to draw a picture of the dress you'd fit into
if it weren't for the snacks you keep around the house for the kids.

Use this space to draw a comic of your extended family ruining yet another Thanksgiving.

Use this space to keep track of all of your
Black/Jewish/Gay friends.

_____

_____

_____

Use this space to list your favorite civil rights leaders.
(And because "Martin Luther King, Jr." doesn't take up much
room, use the rest to write a shopping list for an "ethnic" meal, like
Taco Tuesday or mac-and-cheese with that funny sounding
hot dog that is Spanish or Italian or something, but boy is it
spicy so have a glass of peenogreege on ice ready!)

_____

_____

_____

_____

_____

_____

_____

_____

_____

_____

_____

_____

Use this space to keep track of the books you read (or at least skim) for Book Club, and what you object to about each of them.

Use this space to list the ways you know better than your doctor.

Use this space to write about why you would do a better job
teaching your children than their teachers do.

Use this space to write about why you aren't a feminist.

Use this space to record the ways your Christmas was ruined by the phrase "Happy Holidays."

Karen

Use this space to try to explain the differences between Kwanzaa and Ramadan.

_____

_____

_____

Use this space to list all the reasons to call 911 on a white person.

_____

_____

_____

Use this space to list all the reasons to call 911 on a non-white person.

_____

_____

_____

_____

_____

_____

_____

_____

_____

_____

_____

_____

_____

_____

_____

PUT THE KAREN BACK IN CHRISTMAS!

The joyless libs are on a crusade to deprive good Americans of every traditional celebration they possibly can. Use these clues to name the various holiday sorties God-fearing citizens engage in every year.

Down

1 _____ on Kwanzaa
2 _____ on National Cheeseburger Day
3 _____ on Oktoberfest
7 _____ on Arbor Day

Across

4 _____ on Spring Break
5 _____ on Yom Kippur
6 _____ on Columbus Day
8 _____ on Christmas
9 _____ on March Madness

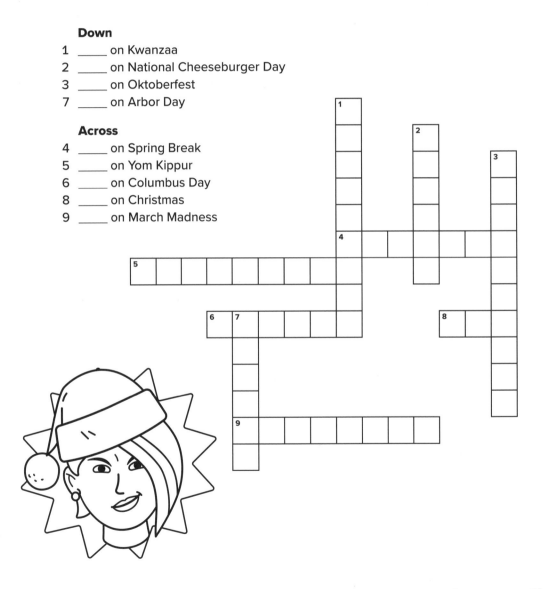

Answers on p. 101

CONNECT THE DOTS...

to discover what your government has been keeping from you!

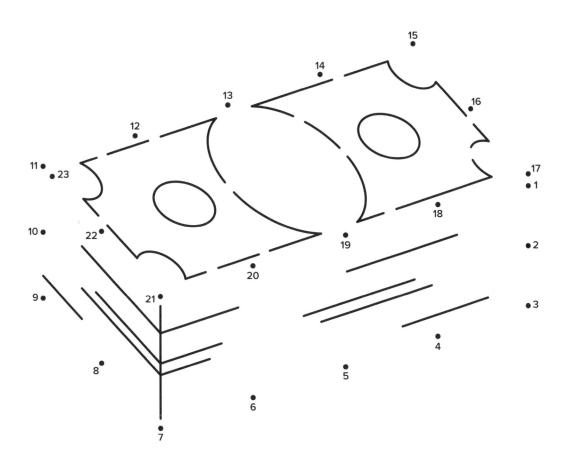

CLUE

Your taxes are being used by welfare recipients to get tattoos!

Answer on p. 101

WHAT'S WRONG WITH THIS PICTURE?

A Quiet Evening at Home

ANSWERS: The man is a nurse and the woman is a doctor; the couch has fewer than 40 throw pillows on it; the dog is a rescue; they are reading books instead of watching TV; there are no crosses burning on their lawn

CROSS-BITCH

Use this cross-stitch pattern to Karen-up your home!

MULTI-LEVEL MARKETING

Karen wants to supplement Kevin's income but doesn't him to
know as it will emasculate him. Can you help her quietly recruit 10 of her
fellow Mompreneurs to sell a collection of needlessly expensive
kitchen tools to their friends and families?

Answers on p. 101

PIN THE MASK ON KEVIN

Just because you're supposed to do something doesn't mean
you should, especially if you feel it infringes on your constitutional rights.
Live free or die, right? (Maybe both!) This game is ideal for guests
of all ages attending anti–social distancing parties.

1. Cut out the masks on page 77.

2. Tape Kevin's all-American face to a wall and insert pins into the mask-shaped pieces.

3. Take a dose of hydroxychloroquine and blindfold yourself.

4. Try to pin the . . . just kidding—there's no way Kevin's wearing a mask!

   Bonus Activity for your Crafting Club:
   Use the extra mask-shapes to create more excuses for Kevin!

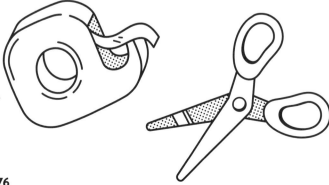

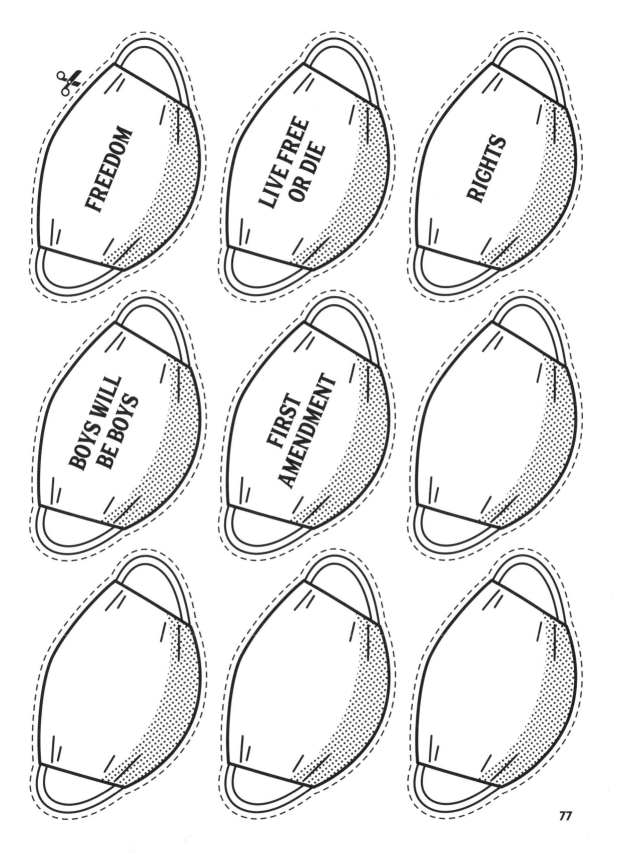

FREEDOM

LIVE FREE OR DIE

RIGHTS

BOYS WILL BE BOYS

FIRST AMENDMENT

KAREN'S HAPPY HOUR WORD SEARCH

```
H  T  Y  A  S  S  T  E  P  N  Y  V  T  E  S  P  S  E  E
U  A  A  P  P  L  E  T  I  N  I  O  R  S  K  T  W  S  S
N  M  C  P  T  I  A  S  E  N  A  K  O  L  E  L  M  U  L
V  O  H  O  M  A  N  T  E  K  O  L  L  R  J  R  P  A  R
Y  V  A  K  P  A  E  A  J  N  F  M  L  M  P  B  E  J  M
H  L  R  S  O  A  N  U  C  G  M  P  G  B  S  A  E  B  B
S  U  C  T  A  N  F  B  U  O  O  F  Q  U  L  A  N  U  U
I  O  H  C  E  I  N  R  A  M  L  D  B  F  L  D  O  E  F
H  A  A  G  U  Y  A  S  O  F  C  A  A  V  I  H  G  N  Q
A  H  R  S  M  L  E  W  R  Z  I  Y  D  D  E  D  R  N  D
R  R  D  C  E  N  R  S  P  S  E  T  E  A  G  A  E  A  Y
D  C  O  O  P  O  N  I  M  O  A  N  A  N  E  N  E  H  U
S  A  N  G  R  I  A  E  X  T  P  P  M  I  N  A  G  R  A
E  S  N  M  E  T  F  J  N  G  S  Y  F  A  T  E  E  K  E
L  V  A  O  O  W  C  H  S  E  L  K  O  O  R  K  L  I  O
T  S  Y  O  M  V  O  T  A  S  S  P  W  E  F  G  E  R  M
Z  O  H  I  B  A  S  K  E  K  O  K  L  R  E  R  P  N  E
E  A  P  O  S  O  M  E  T  H  I  N  G  S  W  E  E  T  R
R  S  H  O  M  A  O  T  G  B  O  L  L  F  E  H  N  R  O
```

chardonnay	pina colada
appletini	something sweet
peenogreege	sangria
cosmo	hard seltzer
frozen marg	PSL

Answers on p. 101

Do you remember what
five words were on page 33?
Only stable geniuses will!
List them here:

1. _____

2. _____

3. _____

4. _____

5. _____

PUT BABY WHERE HE BELONGS!

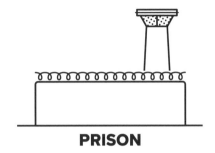
PRISON

BORDER CONTROL CENTER

DAYCARE

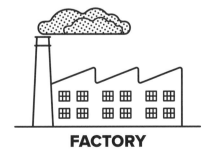
FACTORY

WHAT'S WRONG WITH THIS PICTURE?

CROSS-BITCH

Use this cross-stitch pattern to Karen-up your home!

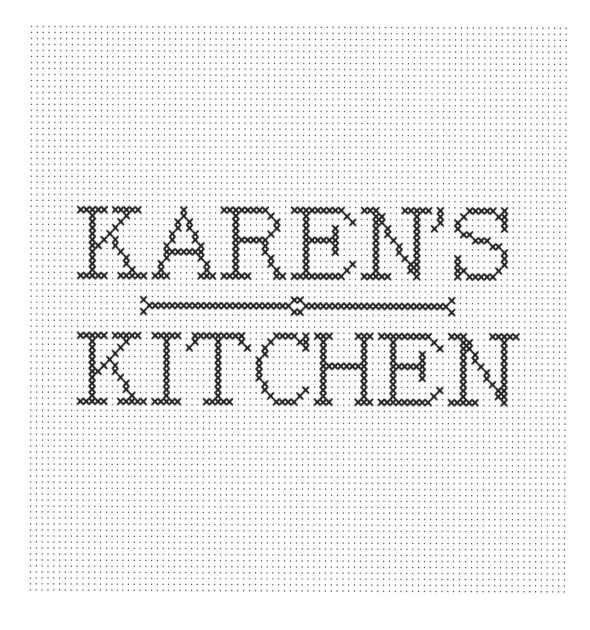

A 'MURICAN 'MERGENCY

It's never been harder to be a white woman than it is today. Threats are everywhere you look—if you look for them in people who don't look like you! Use these clues to identify some suspicious actions to keep an eye out for, which may be 911-worthy when performed by those who don't belong and/or make you vaguely uncomfortable for reasons you are under no obligation to justify.

Down

1 in a car
2 a movie
3 on a phone
5 in a restaurant
6 down a street
8 before a game
9 on a park bench

Across

4 the mail
7 to a friend
9 waiting for the light to change
10 on the subway
11 to music

Answers on p. 102

MATH IS HARD!

Which is why we let Kevin handle our finances, and why he lets our accountant (who just so happens to be Jewish) do our taxes. But sometimes two plus two equals more than the sum of its parts! Put away your calculators and give the scientific method a rest as you solve these problems using only your gut and common sense.

1 If Karen has two unvaccinated children, and those children have a total of 54 unvaccinated classmates, how many of the school's 600 students will die of preventable childhood diseases before herd immunity develops?

Answer: As long as my kids are okay it doesn't matter.

2 If Kevin's commute takes 30 minutes, he cuts off two vehicles every 1.5 minutes, and each vehicle holds two people, how many people will have been victims of Kevin's road rage by the time he reaches home?

Answer: Kevin is the real victim here—they shouldn't have been in his way in the first place.

3 If Kevin attends Kevin Jr.'s baseball games four nights a week, how many volunteer coaches will he threaten with violence over the course of the season?

Answer: As many as it takes to make sure Kevin Jr. gets a trophy.

If Karen and Kevin live on a cul-de-sac with six houses, each of which holds four people, how many minorities would have to move in before they put their house on the market? **4**

Answer: It depends how thick the new neighbors' accents are and whether or not they go into their backyards.

Bonus: How much will they try to shave off the Realtor's commission by claiming the house sells itself?

Answer: 25%. What are you gonna do about it?

5 If it takes six people five days to erect a statue of Christopher Columbus, and two people ten minutes to take it down, how many hurt feelings will Kevin have when he realizes none of this is about him?

Answer: Kevin's feelings are buried too deep to count.

6

If the dinner Karen and Kevin are hosting for Kevin's new boss, Priyanka Patel, lasts three hours, and Karen drinks one glass of chardonnay in the first hour and two every hour after that, how many minutes will pass before Karen asks whether Priyanka's marriage was arranged?

Answer: The real question is how Priyanka expected Karen to know that shrimp scampi wasn't vegetarian! (They're not meat!)

7

If Karen watches two Christmas-themed TV movies every day from November 1 through December 31, how many days will she have to watch before seeing one Black person?

Answer: Six—or only three if you count the time the dog sat on the remote control and changed the channel to BET.

8

How many likes will Kayleigh get if she posts a selfie giving a "peace" sign at her grandma's funeral?

Answer: OMG, like, literally hundreds.

If Karen enters a state of denial each time she hears Rachel Maddow present a fact she doesn't like, how long will it take her to travel all 50 states after watching a week's worth of *The Rachel Maddow Show*?

Answer: Trick question! MSNBC is blocked by the parental controls and Karen can't figure out how to switch them off (the kids know, but they make fun of her every time she has trouble with tech, so it's best to leave well enough alone).

Bonus (assuming Kevin Jr. has disabled the parental controls): How long will it take if the show is guest hosted by Joy Reid?

Answer: I don't really know her. But I'd like to touch her hair.

If Kevin Jr. stays in the closet until he's done with college and moves to a big city, how many times between the ages of 13 and 21 will he try bargaining with God to make him straight?

Answer: Two per year, plus four for each game of "shirts and skins" he plays with the just-out-of-seminary assistant coach while practicing for state championships.

NAME THE MAN

Put a name to the face!

A. Kevin
B. Carlos
C. Juan

A. Antonio
B. Kevin
C. Guido

A. Jean-Luc
B. Marcel
C. Kevin

A. Jesus
B. Kevin
C. Emmanuel

KEVIN'S SUNDAY WORD SEARCH

```
G I D U S M U J D O Z B R E W
W H S X G T H D L V J W S T O
S M T P V X B L G K I S I S H
J L O D R B D T E L P J X L L
O D U I F N R Z C K A A P K Y
J N T G H T D E E O F H A O G
T P B J I C S A W F K A C Y U
D F U D Z B L V B S I T K C Q
P S Z U E E Q H T S K V W N J
P X R B C L F W U S N I X A U
K F S E R V L S F N L E L S Z
B A L E N J A I N A H R O N R
I I Q R W E G P H Z N T P Z N
Y B M Q Y E E R F J Q M K E G
F W S C A W R X E S T P C I S
```

six pack   lager
beer   IPA
brew   stout
brewski   keg
ale   DUI

Answers on p. 102

CROSS-BITCH

Use this cross-stitch pattern to Karen-up your home!

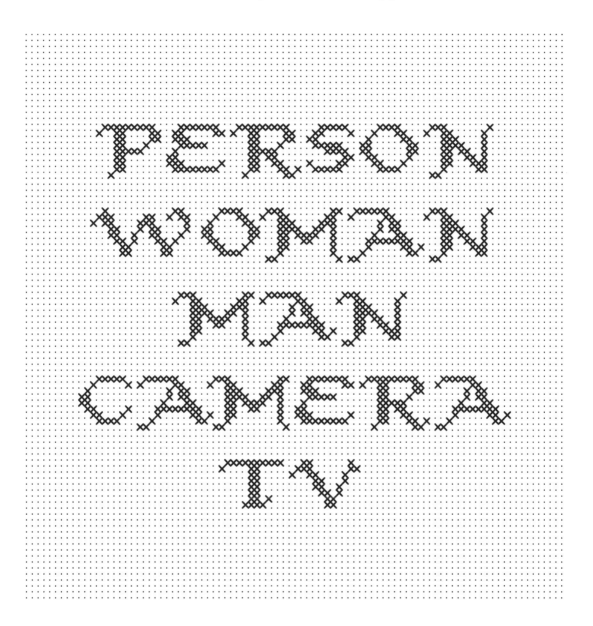

ANSWERS

p. 4

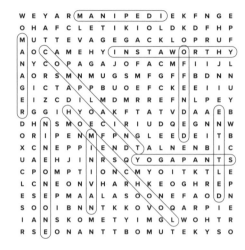

p. 5

CUSTOMER SERVICE

p. 11

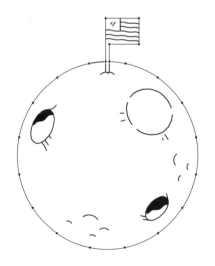

p. 15

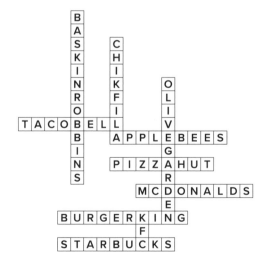

ANSWERS

p. 16–17

cakes   cakes
pray   pray
love   love
children   children
safe   safe
taxes   taxes
flag   flag
say   say
opinion   opinion
wear   wear

p. 18

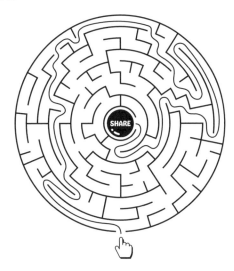

p. 19

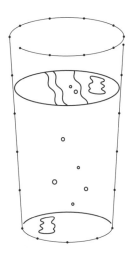

p. 27

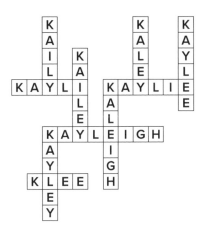

ANSWERS

p. 32

```
H C B S S U T K P N Z V B E C
N A S K E T M M A N U P R A X
B M O P T R U C K P O S O W P
S O P D S A D T C L O J M L N
O V U K F V H Z C J F Q L K C
N P E G O T Z M C O L P A N O
U V B T I B S E A K P A D Y D
E F H D A I B V R N E D K F Q
H S W A M I Q R G M C Y A O S
N X R N F L L W O S E I O O K
A R B E G N K G P N K R E T Z
N A B E P L G I A O H D K B E
B S Q R W T G B N T N D E A N
M A N C A V E R T J E M K L G
K W S P C W A V S E C O Z L S
```

p. 34

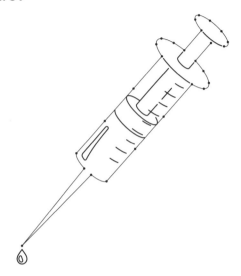

p. 40

p. 41

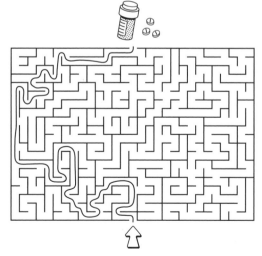

ANSWERS

p. 70

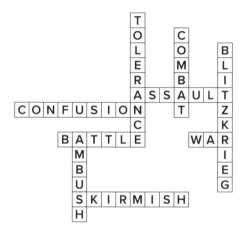

p. 71

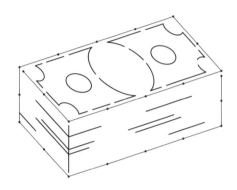

p. 75

p. 81

ANSWERS

p. 87

p. 96

OFFENSIVE LIB-LOVING ORGS TO NOT SUPPORT

The world is filled with nonprofit organizations trying to provide everyone with what Karen is entitled to. The following list includes some of the most egregious, with descriptions adapted from their very own websites. Just make sure to clear your browser history after visiting them—you don't want the secret cabals spying on you to think you're not doing your best to make America great.

———————

❏ **The American Association of People with Disabilities** (AAPD) advocates for full civil rights for the over 60 million Americans with disabilities by promoting equal opportunity, economic power, independent living, and political participation.

aapd.com

❏ **The American Civil Liberties Union** works in the courts, legislatures, and communities to defend and preserve the individual rights and liberties guaranteed to all people in this country by the Constitution and laws of the United States.

aclu.org

❏ **The Audre Lorde Project** is a Lesbian, Gay, Bisexual, Two Spirit, Trans, and Gender Non-Conforming People of Color center for community organizing, focusing on the New York City area.

alp.org

❏ **The Black Farmers Collective** believes the key to a more sustainable, equitable future for communities of color requires eliminating food scarcity and undoing the commoditization of the food industry.

blackfarmerscollective.com

❏ **Black Lives Matter** seeks to eradicate white supremacy and build local power to intervene in violence inflicted on Black communities by the state and vigilantes.

blacklivesmatter.org

❏ **Color of Change** moves decision-makers in corporations and government to create a more human and less hostile world for Black people in America.

colorofchange.org

❏ **The Cupcake Girls** provides confidential support to those involved in the sex industry, as well as trauma-informed outreach, intensive care management, holistic resources, and referral services to provide prevention and aftercare to those affected by sex trafficking.

thecupcakegirls.org

❏ **The David Bohnett Foundation** is committed to improving society through social activism.

bohnettfoundation.org

❏ **Delivering Good** unites retailers, manufacturers, foundations, and individuals to support people affected by poverty and tragedy.

delivering-good.org

❏ **Disabled American Veterans** provides a lifetime of support for veterans of all generations and their families.

dav.org

❏ **Doctors Without Borders** is an international humanitarian organization providing medical services to people in need around the world.

doctorswithoutborders.org

❏ **The Equal Justice Initiative** is committed to ending mass incarceration and excessive punishment in the United States, to challenging racial and economic injustice, and to protecting basic human rights for the most vulnerable people in American society.

eji.org

❏ **Fairness and Accuracy in Reporting** offers well-documented criticism of media bias and censorship and advocates for greater diversity in the press by scrutinizing media practices that marginalize public interest, minority and dissenting viewpoints.

fair.org

❏ **First Book** aims to remove barriers to quality education for all kids by making everything from new, high-quality books and educational resources to sports equipment, winter coats, snacks, and more affordable to its member network of more than 475,000 educators who exclusively serve kids in need.

firstbook.org

❑ **GLBTQ Legal Advocates & Defenders** works to create a just society free of discrimination based on gender identity and expression, HIV status, and sexual orientation.

glad.org

❑ **God's Love We Deliver** improves the health and well-being of men, women and children living with HIV/AIDS, cancer, and other serious illnesses by alleviating hunger and malnutrition.

glwd.org

❑ **Greenpeace** is a global, independent campaigning organization that uses peaceful protest and creative communication to expose global environmental problems and promote solution that are essential to a green and peaceful future.

greenpeace.org

❑ **Habitat for Humanity** builds strength, stability, and self-reliance in partnership with people and families in need of decent and affordable homes.

habitat.org

❑ **The Human Rights Campaign** strives to end discrimination against LGBTQ people and realize a world that achieves fundamental fairness and equality for all.

hrc.org

❏ **The International Rescue Committee** helps people whose lives and livelihoods are shattered by conflict and disaster to survive, recover, and regain control of their future.

rescue.org

❏ **Lambda Legal** works to address the highest priority needs of members of the LGBTQ+ community and those living with HIV.

lambdalegal.org

❏ **The Loveland Foundation** is committed to showing up for communities of color in unique and powerful ways, with a particular focus on Black women and girls.

thelovelandfoundation.org

❏ **The Malala Fund** breaks down the barriers preventing more than 130 million girls around the world from going to school.

malala.org

❏ **The Marsha P. Johnson Institute** protects and defends the human rights of Black transgender people by organizing, advocating, and creating an intentional community to heal, develop transformative leadership, and promote our collective power.

marshap.org

❏ **The My Brother's Keeper Alliance** leads a national call to action focused on building safe and supportive communities for boys and young men of color where they feel valued and have clear pathways to opportunity.

obama.org/mbka

- **NARAL Pro-Choice America** works to protect abortion access across the country, ensure that women can control their own destinies by having access to affordable contraception, hold anti-choice politicians accountable, and demand lawmakers trust women.

  prochoiceamerica.org

- **The National Alliance on Mental Illness** (NAMI) provides advocacy, education, support and public awareness so that all individuals and families affected by mental illness can build better lives.

  nami.org

- **The National Association for the Advancement of Colored People** seeks to ensure a society in which all individuals have equal rights without discrimination based on race.

  naacp.org

- **The National Disability Rights Network (NDRN)** includes agencies in every state and US territory providing legal protection and advocacy services to individuals with disabilities, and member programs work to improve the lives of people with disabilities by ensuring access and accountability in health care, education, employment, housing, transportation, voting, and within the justice system.

  ndrn.org

❏ **The National Organization for Women** is the largest organization of feminist grassroots activists in the United States, taking action through intersectional grassroots activism to promote feminist ideals, lead societal change, eliminate discrimination, and achieve and protect the equal rights of all women and girls in all aspects of social, political, and economic life.

now.org

❏ **The Planetary Society** empowers the world's citizens to advance space science and exploration.

planetary.org

❏ **Planned Parenthood** is a trusted health care provider, an informed educator, and a passionate advocate that delivers vital reproductive health care, sex education, and information to women, men, and children worldwide.

plannedparenthood.org

❏ **The Pop Culture Hero Coalition** creates mental health and bullying prevention programs—using stories we love—for pop culture events, schools, and use at home.

popculturehero.org

❏ **ProPublica** is an independent, nonprofit newsroom that exposes abuses of power and betrayals of the public trust by government, business, and other institutions, using the moral force of investigative journalism to spur reform through the sustained spotlighting of wrongdoing.

propublica.org

- **RAINN (Rape, Abuse, and Incest National Network)** is the nation's largest anti-sexual violence organization. It operates the National Sexual Assault Hotline and also carries out programs to prevent sexual violence, help victims, and ensure that perpetrators are brought to justice.

  rainn.org

- **The Refugee and Immigrant Center for Education and Legal Services** defends the rights of immigrants and refugees, empowers individuals, families, and communities, and advocates for liberty and justice.

  raicestexas.org

- **The Southern Poverty Law Center** is dedicated to fighting hate and bigotry and to seeking justice for the most vulnerable members of our society.

  splcenter.org

- **The Sylvia Rivera Law Project** works to guarantee that all people are free to self-determine their gender identity and expression, regardless of income or race, and without facing harassment, discrimination, or violence.

  srlp.org

- **The Trevor Project** provides crisis intervention and suicide prevention services to LGBTQ young people.

  thetrevorproject.org

❏ **The Transgender Law Center** employs a variety of community-driven strategies to keep transgender and gender nonconforming people alive, thriving, and fighting for liberation.

transgenderlawcenter.org

❏ **The Transgender Legal Defense & Education Fund** is committed to ending discrimination based upon gender identity and expression and to achieving equality for transgender people through public education, test-case litigation, direct legal services, and public policy efforts.

transgenderlegal.org

❏ **True Colors United** implements innovative solutions to youth homelessness that focus on the unique experiences of LGBTQ young people.

truecolorsunited.org

❏ **UN Women** is the United Nations entity dedicated to gender equality and the empowerment of women. A global champion for women and girls, UN Women works with governments and civil society to design laws, policies, and programs that benefit women and girls worldwide.

unwomen.org

❏ **UNICEF** works with governments, civic leaders, celebrities, corporations, campus groups, churches, teachers, and anyone willing to help advocate for the survival and well-being of every child.

unicefusa.org

❏ **The Veteran's Voices Writing Project** enables military veterans to experience solace and satisfaction through writing.

veteransvoices.org

❏ **Vote Run Lead** trains barrier-breaking women to unleash their political power, run for office, and transform American democracy.

voterunlead.org

❏ **When We All Vote** seeks to increase participation in every election and close the race and age voting gap by changing the culture around voting, harnessing grassroots energy, and through strategic partnerships to reach every American.

whenweallvote.org

❏ **World Central Kitchen** was founded by Chef Jose Andres to use the power of food to heal communities and strengthen economies in times of crisis and beyond.

wck.org

❏ **The Wounded Warrior Project** honors and empowers Wounded Warriors who incurred a physical or mental injury, illness, or wound in military service on or after September 11, 2001.

woundedwarriorproject.org